WITCH

By Lisa Kendrick

Dedicated to all the 'witchy' women out there: to every girl told to smile more, to every woman told 'she doesn't have what it takes,' to every gender who has ever been told to 'take it like a man,' to the millions of witches who came before us and the millions who will follow after us.

"We were the people who were not in the papers. We lived in the blank white spaces at the edges of print. It gave us more freedom. We lived in the gaps between the stories." — Margaret Atwood,

May we not only live on the pages, but color all over them.
#METOO

Graphic Design
By Chris Felan

Poems and writings herein are the products of List M. Kendrick, who is responsible for these contents. Wider Perspectives Publishing reserves 1st run of printing rights, but all materials reverts to property of the author at time of delivery. All rights to republication of items inside thereafter revert to the author and she may submit items to contests and anthologies at will.

1st run released 2018 Hampton Roads, Virginia

Copyright © 2018 Lisa Kendrick
All rights reserved.

1st Edition ISBNs -13: 978-1985344334,   -10: 1985344335

2nd Edition 2020, ISBN: **978-1-952773-02-0**

WITCH

Women have found themselves in a position in which they are unfairly labelled, continuously generalized, and contemptuously degraded into two dimensional images. I have long been a feminist, but that process is an evolution. Social constructs take years to digest and break apart and reform into something cognitively viable. When women began so loudly breaking their silences in the fall of 2017, I knew it was time to share my evolution.

In compiling these poems, I realized they clearly reflected my own acceptance and then rebellion of the roles hoisted upon me by society. I was raised in a conservative and religious family that valued virginity above all else until marriage. Therefore, in my world, women were always categorized as 'virgins' (the ideal), 'sluts' (an open expression of sexuality), or 'bitches' (a repression of love and sexuality). Many of my poems in this compilation show the confusion women, squished into two-dimensional beings by patriarchal societies, experience as they struggle to understand the reality of the multi-dimensional processes of love and sexuality.

TABLE OF CONTENTS

6

Virgin

Women as bastions of virginity is a traditional ideal upheld by many contemporary religions. The 'Virgin Mary' has been revered for about 2,000 years in a growing number of civilizations from late Rome to present-day United States. The last 2,000 years have seen a bevy of laws enacted to keep women under the thumb of a patriarchal system. After all, before genetic testing, the only way males could feel certain that women would bear offspring fathered by them was to literally lockdown women's sexual freedoms, first policing girls via their fathers and then via their husbands.

In recent years, a more accurate history of ancient humanity has come to light. Today, there is much evidence to support the idea that early humans worshipped female deities, that women practiced sexual and reproductive freedoms, and that women were originally providers alongside males rather than a submissive and dependent gender.

It is a sad fact that today, millions of women, even in 'democratic' nations, suffer from inequality, assault, abuse, and psychological damage via cultures and religions that uphold archaic patriarchal traditions. In my experiences, many women have been so long brainwashed that they keep their own figurative sisters in chains: blocking access to birth control, making excuses for dangerous male behavior, and denying women rights over their own bodies both figuratively and literally.

Even those of us who defy patriarchal ideals are still influenced by the concepts forced upon us in societies built on inequality. Many women teeter in confusion about love, sex, marriage, motherhood and what we really want if we can ever truly manage to strip away societal expectations. Expecting women to be pure and men to be heroic causes nothing but dysfunction and confusion. Straight women are pressured to marry and to have kids, then treated like pariahs if they cannot live up to expectation.

Songbirds

gilded cage
tissue lined stage—
    feathered wingtips clipped
    curled pinions sheared—
        golden chains dangling
        delicate wrists hanging—
            tang of bars rusted
            reek of wounds salted—
                hushed murmuring
                plumage rustling—
            freedom eradicated
            songbird wasted—
        heartbroken from begging
        throat raw from crying—
    goddess liveried
    prisoner pitied—
gilded cage
tissue lined stage—

Dog Days

Your love was like a tsunami,
beating upon my window panes,
spitting pine needles into my brick facade,
and tipping over my rafters like dominoes.

Then you went silent—
stillness after the maelstrom
without even a draft to tickle my wind chimes.

Your love like rain during the dog days
when clouds build on the horizon
then arrive in a blitzkrieg of booms,
beginning in a fury, but then signifying nothing,
drifting into a drizzle that barely wets doormats.

Your diminishing assault makes
a mockery of the tidal wave your love was before,
makes me regret the time I spent sandbagging
my doorways and taping up my windows.

Becky

Becky is golden locks
that sway in perfect waves
halfway down her straight back.

Becky is owl-like eyes
the color of the sky on a perfect fall day.
Becky is a slim silhouette who still manages
to fall out of all her bras.

Becky is head cheerleader,
the lead in the play,
the saucy blonde at the bar who every male watches.

Becky is the token bombshell CEO
in every business office
who puts on glasses to lead meetings,
short skirts to get promotions,
and dagger glances to slay competitors.

Becky is the childhood darling
of at least one of your ex-boyfriends.

Becky haunts American females,
stalks our cosmetic choices,
stakes claims on our lovers,
and commercially she is called Barbie,
but we may have called her
Emily or Heather or Katelyn or Amy.

Becky is held captive too,
our culture has woven its curse upon her,
contracted her to slay

individuality in countless girls
and to raise jealousy in more women
than will ever admit to it—

damning every Becky
to an unwanted spotlight,
a stereotypical pedestal,
that even Becky must yearn to topple.

Boy's Bathroom

What was she thinking
on that bathroom floor?

That doing favors for spoilt little boys
would be fun and gain her popularity?

Did she not cringe at the germs
squashed beneath her knees—
at the proximity her young body was
to strange boy's shit stains?

Did she not care that what she did
took the sexual revolution back one hundred years?

The rumors of her actions flew faster
than her footsteps down the school's hallways.

For it she was expelled
while he was not,
yet she is the one who
must not know her worth.

What are we thinking,
raising girls who believe they owe
boys favors on bathroom floors?

Breech

You were once a dream
      of which my feelings conceived,

      but your vision is so narrow
          our discourse has become laborious,

a process of birth in which
      new thoughts are all breech:

      if we can't let innovation
          become a fluid movement,

moving forward will leave us
      bleeding out on the table.

Coffee House Spectacle

They look alike as so many couples do
after marriage has molded them.

In the bustling coffee shop they commandeer a table,
tiny tot in tow, enthroned in a carrier Cadillac.

They resonate 'ideal American family':
tall and lithe, smooth hair, blue eyes, brand-name clothing.

For one moment I envy their perfection,
their apparent familial bliss.

Ten minutes into coffee, she begins volleying
angry staccato sentences across the table at him—

In one split second they go from perfect threesome
to a coffee house spectacle that makes me blush.

Suddenly cups of gourmet java are shoved to the side
as they gather their things in furious spasms.

He turns at the last second to grab the now shrieking child,
following the wake of her angry strides and fearsome glance.

They exit chaotically, a wake of confusion left
floating behind the muted scream of a steam wand.

Elaine

On an island in the middle of a stream
Colorific magic falls in the guise of leaves
Yet in a turreted castle, a princess mourns her lover,
Who, like the summer, fled her hearth months ago.

Sunsets drown the castle in red-gold
While her son plays in the drowsy garden below,
But the forsaken princess only mourns the road
That twists into the gloomy distance.

Her husband had been a glamorous knight,
Tipping his helmet and jousting in her name,
Lavishing her with promises all those years ago,
Then taking her soul hostage on his charger
As he fled her bed to serve his king.

Night falls as leaves shrivel and blow away,
Winter reaches out tentative fingers
As a funeral barge breaks its moorings
To float downstream to Camelot.

A child left motherless, a knight's word broken,
His decisions demanding their fare—
Once innocence lost from a steadfast heart,
Neither grace nor fury can change
The courses set and futures lost.

Guinevere

Ivory sheets entangled from passion,
Dawn gleaming through windowpanes,
Summer unfurling in wildflowers and singing larks.

Soon autumn takes summer's place—
Reigning in deeper colors and wilder winds,
and with the dying leaves twists a devil's journey.

Clandestine lovers make the most of nights,
Girded with guilt while hiding grins
Till time dwindles and freedoms end.

Then in wintry glades and shuttered rooms they meet,
Too late to purge their bodies of each fervid touch—
The truth will free them and break their world apart.

A valiant knight, a torrid human in the end,
The king's trusted friend from legend slips away,
Leaving behind the things he could not conquer.

A queen mourns the chains that bind her,
The dregs of love taken out of its place,
Living on when she would rather die.

Spilled Milk Heartbreak

the dribbles,
viscous and white,
are not always harmless,
some can scald like acid,
eradicating worlds
as it puddles—

forming event horizons,
disintegrating elements
and recreating shadows
of those atoms in a galaxy
light years away—

fabricating a gollum
of you, a pitiable creature
with palsied hands,
who will never dare
pour milk again—

A Child to Break Us

Slowly things fell apart,
events started tripping
over themselves as we matured,
time culling out the undergrowth
as our reaching branches
began battling for space,
sparring for sunlight and water,
our chloroplasts warring for dominance.

Rooted to the forest floor,
there is little territory for stretching boughs
and spreading leaflets, so we had a child
to rein in our separate expansions,
thinking offshoots would stunt growth,
germination would halt advancement,
and multiplication would cancel division.

Only then things fell apart more quickly,
a forest fire of evolution,
decimating the entire woodland—
offspring finishing what nature had initiated,
splintering both of us apart into kindling.

How Do You Know?

How do you know when it's time to get a divorce?
I Googled it today because no bookstore carried such a manual.

It was easy to find self-help books for other aspects of
relationships:
Everything from *Tantric Sex for Dummies*
To *How to Catch and Keep Your Man,*
But, apparently, no one had bothered writing a book
About when to call marriage quits and seek solace elsewhere.

I found some new techniques for masturbation,
That he and I are at opposite ends of the 'language of love'
spectrum,
And that we both 'stonewall' when we fight, which we do
daily, But nothing could list the stages of marital endings
Or how to bring it to a close in an amicable fashion
Rather than like trailer trash in bitter fights on the back lawn.

Do you leave when he he'd rather have a beer than talk to you?
Do you leave when he stops looking at you with any
tenderness? Do you leave when he downloads so much porn he
crashes the computer?
Do you leave when you can no longer remember what love was
once like?
Can you leave then, or is it still a cop out?

No printed self-help manual would tell me,
Nothing could offer any commercialized form of advice,
While the one person who was once my bastion
Snores indifferently thousands of miles away across the
hallway In the bedroom I moved out of months ago.

Matrimonial Death

Everyone knows the first step is denial.
Pretense shrouds every response—
We pass like spirits through one another
Sharing the same space,
Yet our realms of influence
Spiral steadily away
Until nothing of our essences embraces,
And nothing of what 'we once were' resonates.

Anger briskly sets in once denial has slithered away.
Every image becomes drenched in scarlet—
Our words dripping blood
Upon the spotless carpet—
Every utterance evoking betrayal,
Every touch an alien invasion,
Until we go to great lengths to avoid one another
Splitting apart in the same container like oil and vinegar.

Next bargaining sneaks stealthily in—
things will get better if we seek guidance,
If we bring forth a new life,
If we pretend we are unchanged
And promise to be what we once were,
If we take lovers, just to fill in the gaps,
Everything seems plausible
Once matrimony is in its death throes.

Eventually, depression worms its way in—
All those years wasted,
Promises split asunder,
A part of your soul damned
By the fear that there will never be
Light at the end of the tunnel,
A cat to savor the spilt milk,
Or vindication for marital martyrdom.

Peace is as elusive as nirvana—
Did it fall down the rabbit hole?
Is it in the land that time forgot?
Will things ever be normal again?
Eventually acceptance seeps in between the cracks,
Covertly filling the darkened vacancies,
Until one morning you wake up, take a breath
And realize your lungs and heart are working again.

Cookie Jar

Taking the lid off,
I slide my hands into the round
opening, reaching my fingertips
to touch the ceramic bottom
where not even crumbs are left.

I spent years curbing
the cookie monster inside my chest—
learning to live without the cookies
my parents had never made for me.

Now I check inside the jar,
trying to keep it filled for my children.

I pull down ingredients,
mixing batter as best I can,
fearing the cookies I mix together
from other's discarded recipes
can never be enough to placate
the cookie monsters they may inherit from me.

Abyss

In today's world, we pretend
that 'life' means 'forever',
not the short span it really represents.

But when the first wrinkle appears
on a youthful face, we realize time is slipping,
sliding into an abyss of shorter days
and less options; a fearful precipice.

They lie, those that say
a wrinkle is a sign of wisdom—
a simple laugh line
as if it is a good thing,
this scar of laughter.

What time and mirth created
can be fixed by mankind,
but more will appear,
and gravity waits to pull down
breasts and weight buttocks.

The grains fall too quickly
into that abyss, and I,
stand stalwart, refusing
to take that leap.

riptide

missing you terribly, a flowing
      ache, wild waves of memories,
the most destructive force on earth—

your taste salts my lips, your Burberry cologne
      still on my sheets, high tide sweeping over me,
breakers ripping apart my beachhead—

i reach for the whiskey on the nightstand
      to stymie the flow but i still end up shedding
salty currents, a riptide carrying my heart out to sea—

curling up under the covers, i compose a text,
      a tirade of black lettering on my four inch screen,
but i stop myself before hitting send—

our love, a tsunami into which we bled
      little bits of ourselves, our needs
tumbling over each other in frothy crests—

what began as an intertidal zone, spawning
      the primordial soup of possible creation,
instead became a deadly crosscurrent—

our storm front signaling sharks for a feeding frenzy,
      you, always demanding more time than I had to give,
me, furious you could never respect my creativity—

so i let you go, a part of me wishing i could surrender
      my sands to your erosion, but most of me knowing
we were never going to find a rhythm of ebb and flow—

Slut

Eventually, women with a strong sexual drive break away from the virginal 'ideal'. Many of us are then forced to embrace terms like 'slut.' In this, there is no middle ground in a patriarchal society.

I grew up friends with mostly males, knowing they lusted
for women who were sexual (who they openly called many forms of 'slut,' 'whore,' and 'freak'), but they only wanted to marry a 'good' girl. Many young women I knew maintained the 'good' girl image via any number of falsehoods, some even carefully keeping hymens intact while engaging in other sexual acts.

Additionally, women turn on each other. Some men certainly place women in boxes, but after centuries of conditioning those men do not need to because women can be their own brutal gender police. Study the numbers of women who remain in abusive relationships, who support politicians known for sexual harassment, who point fingers at women for speaking out, who belittle sexually active women, and who block their own gender from political routes to workplace and healthcare access equality.

The brainwashing begins as children. Not only do American women grow up in a world where girls are dressed in pink and given pink 'girly' toys like dolls and kitchen sets, but are also hampered by strict and conservative religions. Certainly, I was told by church leaders that it was my duty to protect my virginity. I was indoctrinated with terrible fables where women were promised a place in heaven as long as they obeyed their fathers, did not tempt men, and chose death over loss of virginity. Even deviating from these ideas in thought, could cost a girl heaven. I was told by my pastor, when I was only twelve, that because I was an attractive girl, I would be tempted by the devil to engage in sex. Per this man, it was my sacred duty to not tempt the males around me. I was reminded that I would damn myself to hell if I touched myself or engaged in sexual behavior outside of the marriage bed and that, even in that bed, it was a mortal sin to practice sodomy or fellatio.

Thousands of American women are raised to similar fables. Almost everyone says boys should be 'morally responsible' too, but simultaneously shrug, shake their heads, and murmur that 'boys will be boys'. Women who want freedom, always find ourselves the brunt of negative terminology and confusion as we try to find who we really want to be. Women who are sexual and who differentiate between sex and love find themselves shut down, confused, or ignored.

Tantric

pooling just beneath
the surface of my
skin, it yearns
to burst forth
using my hands as
tools that record
desires and insights,
spooling through
my head this
burst, coiling and
releasing like
a tantric orgasm

Suicide Bomber

forgotten lover—
an intimate caress
so long forsaken
that its re-entry
is like a bomb
where loneliness
reigned and had
so long expanded
until it felt like something
filled those spaces—

stealthily soft—
a shocking surprise
with the euphoria
of physical fulfillment
riding close behind,
ricocheting through
senses accidentally
abandoned long ago
to a deadening vacancy—

coiled spring—
ratcheted beneath my breasts,
hidden over the phone,
crouched between texts,
balancing thunderously,
threatening to implode,
desperately reining it in
before your attentions
activate my suicidal bomb,
leaving behind
only fragments of me.

Just Friends

I remember how it was—
your touch, euphoric
your kiss, medicinal
your scent, intoxicating,
but not anymore.

You see, we broke
what was once splendid
with our words—
figurative bruises have made
your touch, excruciating
your kisses, unsavory
your scent, repugnant.

Now we are 'just friends'
in theory, all hurts, forgiven
transgressions, pardoned
contracts, retracted.

But our words,
released from their leash
when the first metaphoric
punch was thrown
have transformed us
into strangers,
even to ourselves.

Fiend

I learned about love
at the feet of my mother—
my secrets her weapons,
my kindness her tool to force submission,
her hand raised to slap my face.

I learned about love
by watching my stepfather—
looking past me as if I wasn't there,
disrupting peace on dusky evenings,
his fist raised to punch my mother.

I learned about love
one night at the age of eleven—
when my grandfather came to my rescue,
brandishing a shotgun for special effect,
and I decided love was an ugly fiend
who I could never let raise a hand to me.

Orgasm

Shrugging off the bridle to careen freely,
      taking a mighty leap over the threshold
            to land with an ecstatic jolt,

            wildness careening from arched neck,
      satisfaction cresting in waves
from muscles bunching and releasing,

pheromones detected in delicately flaring nostrils,
      excitement quivering along back and haunches
            to rollick down legs gripping and tightening,

            arrowing down a path that widens into bliss,
      the taste of gratification
escaping through frenetic exhalations,

exertions fading into the beat of a heart.

Sunbathing

the sand,
pressing against my fingertips,
its heat and hardness
a physical presence
that arcs beneath me—

the breeze,
cascading against my skin,
its breathy touch
caressing my hair
teasing my breasts
kissing my thighs—

the sun,
pulsating through me
penetrating every pore,
flushing my skin
a heated pink
causing sweat to run
in sensuous rivulets—

the water,
salty and suggestive
heaving between my legs,
it clasps me against its bosom
as I dunk slowly,
enveloping myself in its salty chill
the relief it brings—

a climax.

Antojos

Eyes pooled
between almond lids
dripping chocolate
sprinkled with red pepper.

Skin bronzed,
steaming café latte
promising the warmth
of buttery toast.

Hair burnished
into chestnut waves,
tawny cascades reminiscent of
earthy espresso.

My mocha Botticelli,
tempting me
across the crowded cafe,
proffering my antojos.

PDA

Control walked out the door that first night—
Lust burned through everything,

Fingers couldn't be stopped from grasping,
And lips from sucking—

Deserted aisles at bookstores,
Corner booths at restaurant,
Parking lots on Sundays,

Recklessness surrounded us—
Common sense surrendered to us,

We existed solely to close
The gap of space between us

Until we had sucked up all the oxygen—
Our blue flame extinguished
More quickly than we had shed clothing.

Falling

Falling into your soul,
I never stopped to check the plunge
or look toward the peaks
your emotions etched into my heart.

Time and time again I had learned
how to stop such falls,
how to check the rage of hormonal imbalance,
how to staunch the flows of souls
speeding toward one another,
how to stop their merging with a cauterizing
pain injected at the precise moment.

Time and time again I had learned
how to stop a fall right before it
could become an avalanche,
right before it could plummet off the cliff.

Yet falling into your soul
I never stopped to check the plunge,
sure of my control, I never checked the lines,
the safety nets were never put in place.

Time and time again I had learned
how to curb the maddening rush
and crawl from ravines unscathed,
yet falling into your soul

I didn't stop to check my gear,
or look up to gauge the peaks,
until it was too late to stop the plunge
of my heart toppling off your cliff.

Mismatch

You demand a tryst like the splendor of the sun—
the source of life around which we must revolve,
the entity that drives us into our elliptical orbits,
the god who feeds our burgeoning chloroplasts.

I need an affair like the serenity of the moon—
an object that exerts force when below the horizon,
a rhythm that pulsates with the ebbing and flowing tides,
a goddess who courts our demons on clear nights.

You demand a tryst that is an all-consuming addiction—
leaving no room for independent contemplation,
a fire that burns up all the oxygen in the room,
restructuring our breaths into anaerobic processes.

I need an affair that is simple, quiet, and deep—
flowing silently beneath our undulating surfaces,
a part and parcel to who we already are,
not something that burns us to crisps and then remakes us.

Exclusivity

Staring at a contract of exclusivity
I turn tail and run rampant into the night
tagging the first stag I stumble across
and taking him down like a clumsy neophyte.

I have become the most dangerous game,
unleashing myself upon the hides of the unwary,
ripping throats were I have no business being,
and marking territories that were never mine.

Terror has me flushing out prey in frenzied agitation
with a maniacal urgency to eviscerate,
resignation pushing me onto the prowl,
despair making the hunted taste rancid.

Staring at a contract of exclusivity,
I regress into a mewling juvenile
unleashing myself upon a naive populace
to frantically savage the first heart I careen into.

Fifty Shades

There is something to be said
　　　for the simplicity of a one night stand—

the heat of attraction in stolen glances
　　　of drunken, back up against the wall passion,

for the gut-wrenching cataclysm of strangers' souls colliding,
　　　but there is also something to be said

———

for the complexity of a long-term lover,
　　　the snarls of emotion sheathing caresses,

of riotous tendrils to grip in passionate exchanges, for silken
　　　ropes wrapping themselves around limbs.

Long Ago

She stopped wanting sex long ago—
        Too many years of an ingrained notion
that sex was dirty and only 'whores' enjoyed it—
        Too many years spent believing
'mothers' don't have sex and only 'sluts' crave it—

She prayed in church and went to work
        and bitched about the small stuff—
He took care of all the tedious things,
        the grass, the trash, the maintenance—
When she shoved him into the extra bedroom
        she told herself that she had done her duty—

Since sexuality and physical intimacy were, to her, carnal sins
        she no longer supplied him, he looked elsewhere—
In her denial she refused to see the shambles of their marriage
        Until he confronted her with packed bags—

She despised him for his needs and for snagging some
'hussy'— She backtracked with harsh threats
because in regard to the care of their offspring
she could hold them both prisoners forever
        so neither could move on—
                so neither could find themselves—
                    so they could live a lie—

Till they both stopped having desires—
        Long ago—

Sex and Love

A girl views
sex and love as
inseparable partners,
an idealistic stupor
where one inexorably
leads into the other
and back again—

a spiraling scenario
if she can only
guide a man along it
and force his hand
by withholding sex
and cajoling love
and then back again.

When I was a girl
I was taught to use sex
as the weapon for love—
as if by assault I could
beget adoration.

Yet adults learn
sex and love are not
the same, that one
does not guarantee the other—

partners do not seek
change or control
but give themselves room
to enjoy sexuality
and stay open to the love
that might grow
of its own accord
between the gaps.

We Tell Ourselves

Nothing is too demeaning for you if it gives you a shot,
Playing nice might stick in your throat like a bloated cock
Till you learn how to overcome your tendency to gag—
Slaves don't have any weapons outside of their own bodies
So learning how to expertly use your personal arsenal
Isn't selling yourself short, it's using your imagination,
So when you fetch him that beer and tolerate the pussy grab
Do it with the knowledge it's the only strategy you've got.

Use every trick in the book without a touch of guilt,
Though it's not the high road, it may be the only one out—
Who cares if Billy Bob is mesmerized by mammary glands,
It's no hardship to you if the swing of your ass earns a tip,
You do not demean yourself by learning to play their game,
They made the rules and gave you all the handicaps
So if a pair of long legs in stilettos helps you survive
Then you might live to see a day your daughters don't have to play.

So fight like hell every day even if it means
Pasting on a smile and serving goddamn sweet tea—
You are never too low for a nicely spun double entendre
Your male peers would as soon kick you as look at you—
You were born into the dogfight, but having a vagina
crippled you at birth— you will hate every insipid insinuation
And you will loathe every moment spent on your back,
You will do it to soothe your opponent enough to expose his neck.

The system is broken into fragments
All the king's men can never put back together again,
That shit has already been fucking detonated
So you have to learn to circumnavigate Humpty-Dumpty
Till under cover of complacency, you instigate a new game
Where the rules aren't even about equality, but equity—
Because getting on your knees to break that glass ceiling
Might really be worth it, if it will free your daughters from slavery.

Bitch

Just as the terms 'virgin' and 'slut' refer to polar opposites and come with a plethora of socially constructed connotations, the term 'bitch' has not fared any better. In the world I have experienced as an adult, there is no place for women to be sexually empowered beings. In adult dating realms, women who aren't either virginal or sexually active, must therefore be unapproachable. Women who don't smile enough, who put careers first, who don't play at being coquettish, who change their minds about offering sexual favors, or who show offense to aggressive males are often referred to as female dogs.

I never liked playing this game, but I simply didn't believe there was another option. I liked going out and I accepted being 'free' came with danger. I kept a knife in my purse. I went to bars in groups of friends when I could. I made sure a friend knew when and where I was on dates. If I went out alone, I made friends with doormen and bartenders and bouncers, so I would have some protection against having a drink drugged or a male openly assaulting me.

I accepted the risk of being date raped as the price of my social and sexual freedom. Socially, I played hardball with the 'players'. I pretended I did not need anything but a good dick and a solid lay. At work, I was a different person: I maintained a strict professional demeanor, but I was still harassed constantly. Everywhere I went for most of my adult life, strange men catcalled me and followed me with lewd suggestions, even sometimes trying to rub themselves against me in public. I laughed it off as long as I could because every woman knows, if you are alone (even in the grocery store), being nice to male aggressors is a safer option, but, eventually, I became too furious to play nice.

I pushed back. I called men out. I treated them like dogs. I raged against straight males. The fact is, I like freedom. I like coming and going as I please. I like having my own place. I wanted a relationship, but even those ended up being about the man's needs and not about my needs. My love life was never a romantic comedy. My love life always left me empty and confused because I had nothing to build my expectations on but unrealistic stereotypes and confusing metaphors.

All women who have fought for options and equality become enraged. To be a feminist in a patriarchal society is to be incensed. Once I stopped hiding it, I couldn't take it back.

Pussy

Some people think spitting bullshit about conquests
makes a boy into man.
They think it funny to brag about 'hitting it'—
to joke about pussy as if it is an animal boys have rights to
violate.

Boys shove responsibility upon pussy,
blame pussy for failure—
expect pussy to validate desire.

Girls are taught to lap disrespect up like spilt milk,
trained to laugh at rape jokes,
to spread their thighs even when boys abuse them—

boys think they own pussy because in this world
females are sluts if they 'give out' and bitches if they do not—
boys think it acceptable to treat females like animals.

The fact is, every American woman will have been raped,
or know someone who has been assaulted, by the age of
twenty—

every American woman will experience sexual harassment
at least once in her profession—

every American woman will have to call
a lover, a bouncer, a brother, or a father
to save her from the attentions of an ill-behaved boy,
some boy who thinks pussy was made for him.

This problem is an epidemic—
it is a crime women spend their entire lives

fearing empty hallways,
avoiding dark corners,
wary of crowded dance floors,
safeguarding drinks,
making friends with bouncers,
mapping escape routes,
taking friends for protection,
pretending to have a boyfriend,
playing nice to stave off aggression,
knowing walking down the street is a risk,
being alone, a gamble,
getting into someone's car, Russian roulette.

Imagine living like that and you will realize
spitting bullshit about conquests does not make a boy a man.

It is never funny to brag about 'hitting it'—
pussy is not some stray feline
boys have any right to claim.

No Big Deal

A guy said to me,
about a snippet from a woman comedian
who joked that at 160 pounds
she could 'still get dick'.

He said, "160 pounds is no big deal, and besides,
the fact that she is female gives her access
to more sexual opportunity."

Pause—
Count fucking backwards
and inhale—

160 pounds is a death knell if you're a female in the public eye.

Do men have any clue what some women go through
or what it's like to have an eating disorder like anorexia?

It never completely goes away.

All those models I worshipped in my teens,
the years I never let myself have more than 800 calories a day
and then I'd still felt like a beached fucking whale.

In twenty years I have not looked at a scale—
If I do, I will spiral into a depression
that will not leave until I can count every single rib
because compared to every female image of beauty I have ever
seen I think myself grotesque.

Pause—
Count fucking backwards
and inhale—

So while we're on the subject of beauty
I guess this guy didn't bother to hear her whole shtick
about the irony of a comedic feminist
who was honored by a fashion magazine.

Or how such entities dictate how women feel about themselves
and how their staffs usually make the non-models
feel like buckets of discarded cum.

But I guess he didn't get the sardonic tone in that either
because he has no fucking clue
the humiliation women are made to feel
when they are considered superficially sub-par.

After all, secondary men get fabulous wives all the time,
just look at any sitcom from the 1990's.

Pause—
Count fucking backwards
and inhale—

So, according to this guy,
the fact that I have more 'sexual opportunity'
means men and women are on an equal playing field?

The fact that he keyed in on that point
paints a picture of him,
jealous dog, he got me—
cougar status, anorexia crazy and all,

I can get dick every fucking day
because that's my goal in life,
a diet of penis.

Pause—
Count fucking backwards
and inhale—

What this guy should have picked up on
is the fact that a female comedian can stand up and say the
things she did is a sordid victory.

Maybe she could have said something
more intellectually inspiring.

Maybe we won't be playing that clip for our children,
but she is waging a war in her own way
and battles aren't pretty.

So if any guy doesn't get that,
the least he can do is to shut his fucking mouth
and rejoin the other boys
out on the playground.

Pro-Choice

For pro-lifers argumentation is easy:
throw shame in the faces of women like sand in the face of an
enemy.

The fallacious soldiers of scare tactics and dogmatism
fall in line like experienced Marines trained to kill.

Conservatives contemptuously cower women with images of
infants
and charge them them with the murder of tiny, theoretical
souls.

What pro-lifers like to forget is the true faces of their
opponents:

women, nursing wounds given to them by tyrannical husbands;

wives not allowed birth control yet whose minds
and bodies are beaten by religious demands;

women who have meticulously used every precaution
and know in their souls they cannot raise a child;

young women with no means of support
and no man stepping up to be the father;

teenagers who will be ostracized from families;

women who must make the choice between their bodies and
their lives or that of cells growing inside;

young girls ripped from childhood
by the licentious hands of a family member.

What pro-lifers cannot fathom is the guilty sorrow
already heaped at the feet of these women,
without legal options women have
sought coat hangers in darkened alleyways,
drugs on which to overdose,
and knives with which to open veins.

What pro-lifers cannot abide
are the empathetic medical staff,
professionals willing to risk their lives
because they know abortion is sometimes the only feasible
choice.

The same politicians who block abortions,
block access to birth control, and condone
policies that condemn viable offspring
to the same terrible cycle that brings women in for abortions.

Women who cross that threshold come from
every race,
every economic niche,
every walk of life,
and every one of them is not there on purpose.

So lay your mutilated fetus pictures on the fucking table, and I
will raise you:

tortured souls of terrified young girls,

heartrending cries of battered wives,

broken hearts of women teetering on the edges of breaking
points,

lost innocence of children used against their wills,

and my full house will beat your infantry
of fallacious propaganda every time.

Wine From Her Nipples

If she could pour wine from her nipples,
she would be seized and taxed.

If she could birth manna from her vagina,
she would be forced to feed the wealthy.

Capitalists would line up to wrap her in chains,
to pump her with their mealy sperm,
to force pregnancy upon her again and again.

She would be a concubine for evangelical indulgence:
suckling at her teats and eating her pussy,
coming away with mouths dripping and cocks emptied.

If ever she could pour wine from her nipples,
she would be a slave forever.

Stilettos

I can hear whispering behind my back,
"Look at those heels she is wearing."

As if wearing them is not within my rights,
as if wearing them as been deemed inappropriate by peers, as if
there isn't a price that I have paid to wear them.

I wear them like they are nothing,
but it doesn't mean they don't hurt.

They are a natural fit for me
because I grew up on my toes,
in pink ballet shoes with wooden tips
that I wore until my feet soaked them in blood,
and then I cleaned them out and put them right back on.

These heels?
Well, I don't see my feet bleeding.

I wear them because they make me feel
taller, stronger, braver, younger,
more in charge, less damaged—
well they are worth the pain to me
and that is all that should matter to you.

If, amongst yourselves, you feel the need
to hold yourself my judges
in order to imagine yourself less damaged,
then you will never get it, and may you
never have to walk in shoes like these.

Appellation

"Sweetheart,"
to steady a shying stead
when the bit has failed to curb her.

"Honey,"
to entice a wasp from stinging
when her life has been threatened.

"Sugar,"
to sweeten the bitter dregs
after all the goodness has been drained off.

"Baby doll,"
to quiet the temper of a child
who has been denied equality.

"Princess,"
to offer a pedestal where gilded
edges hide golden shackles.

Damn Girl

"Hey, sweetheart, you are hot!"
These men, I think, are homeless,
sunning themselves on a street corner,
taking in the scenery
before the homeless shelter across town
opens back up for the night.

"Are you Irish, honey?"
These men, I think, are harmless,
seeking refuge on the city sidewalk,
they are the disenfranchised
left to rot by a system that worships a golden calf
and treats dark skin like a disease.

"Damn, girl!"
These men, I think, are not my enemy,
but they are the prime reason
why most of my life
I was afraid to walk on streets alone
and why I have on sweatpants and no makeup.

"I bet nothing ruffles your fine feathers!"
These men, I think, believe they proffer
compliments because I have to say, 'thank you',
and act as if I am appreciative
in case saying what I want to say
turns them into something dangerous.

"Baby, your ass is out of control!"
These men, I think, are better than this,
but I would still like to say, 'fuck you',
yet I cannot face them again,
so I take a different route home
hating myself every step of the way.

Backseat Editor

You say you love me
yet you speak over me
when you don't like
what I have to say.

You say I am your soul mate
yet you backseat drive
as if I am incapable
of navigating my own life—

your condemnation
a criticism of my creativity
because my pointed language
doesn't fit into your lexicon
and its direction
doesn't jibe with your compass.

You claim you don't judge
yet you do with every breath
spewing red marks
across my rough drafts
and spitting advice
I never asked for.

You cannot tolerate
my language playing
in all of the free spaces
between my syntax,

so you speak over
the sounds of my poetry
as it bleeds little pieces of me
all over the floorboards
while you dictate

which road I should take.

I can't have you
pointing fingers
at all the pages of me
you don't want.

I can muzzle my pen but
some part of my inkiness
will always leak out
of the edges to silhouette
the brighter drops of me,
ink trailing behind
like a twisting street.

You cannot love
the pretty sections of me
and ignore all the chapters
you don't like.

You cannot possess me
by calling out
which way direction
I should choose.

You say you love me,
but I'm gonna pull over here
and ask that you
get the fuck out of my car.

Taxidermy

If love is war
then I would rather
be predator than prey.

If love is a hunt
then I would rather
mount the heads of beasts
upon my wall than be
the hunted hart
with an arrow through its neck.

If love is vengeance
then I will breed its species
in my own dark forests
so that I am the only one
to hunt and mount them.

Master

Masterbation: I realized today that I can't spell it.

I was writing an essay about how female masterbation is faux
pas, how female sexuality is seen as degrading,
how I was raised to believe that desire is sinful.

I was typing the word masterbation and watching
that squiggly redness underline it every time,
and I thought, what the fuck?

Spell check doesn't even recognize this word?

Until I checked it out and realized
that even as an 'enlightened' female
I was still putting masculinity into that word,

putting myself into the hands of a 'master'—
a word associated with men who rule.

Even when in the act of something deeply personal
I gave myself a king, an owner, a master
because isn't that what I have been conditioned
to look for in the men around me?

Brainwashed to the point that even I had to learn
to take the master out of masturbation
and claim my sexuality for myself.

Wolf Pack

It is the mall on Saturday
and the women come in droves—

career women in suits and heels,
athletes in shorts and sports bras,
mothers more casual, less svelte—

but everywhere status is obvious.
Even wolves have a system for it
and women are much more savvy
though just as savage as any dog.

Here rank is based on a brand name,
splashed on shoes and purses and tits.

It is in the mall on a Saturday
where women fight for rungs
on an imaginary ladder
the patriarchy holds up for them.

White Privileged Males

Your bullshit is a thunder clap
that sounds in my bosom like a gunshot.

You define contemporary religion,
distort the truth of history books,
deny women equal pay,
demolish all possibility of equitable opportunity,
treat women as inferior individuals –
you made me into an animal
who bears the marks of your shackles.

You should know
it is only the fear of prison bars
keeping me from tripping the locks
and ripping your throat out.

You made me who I am
and I have no ethical boundary
regarding the hide of someone
who has mistreated me my entire life.

You fear the color of someone's skin?
You fear marriage equality dirtying your habits?

What you should fear is me
and all the other white women
who have had the misfortune
of being intimately squished
beneath the heel of your boot.

Sacrament

entails you loving only my brilliance
with none of the dripping darkness
that twirls between the saffron—

it is mock crucifixion held beneath
a tinted spotlight drenching a pedestal
while gyrating shadows frolic at its base—

swallowing your sacrament
would be worse than a fasting penance,
accepting your supplication

would mean sacrificing pieces to fit an image—
heeding your prayers,
would only transform my body into bland wafers

you will offer parishioners
with watered down wine
distilled from my blood—

having faith in me, means
never asking me to ascend your altar,
or to bear your cross.

Convenient Store

Only a ten minute lunch break
in a twelve hour workday
to scan the tiny aisles
and peruse shelves packed
with over-priced items
for something palatable

when I notice you staring
with a hunger that makes my skin crawl.
"Ay, mami, you looking good!"

I carefully stuff diet Slurpee
into its oversized cup and lid
while scrutinizing the yogurt selections
as I avoid the donut display

trying with difficulty to ignore
your eyes assaulting my person.
"Hey, baby, can I help you find anything?"

Pausing to grab a bag of nuts
while comparing bruises on bananas
and weighing dark chocolate options,

your presence an invasion of my space,
my cringing an involuntary motion.
"Goddamn, you just so hot!"

My hands shake as I pay for items,
my legs beat a hasty retreat,
your gaze a hot poker to my backside.

I guess you didn't get the memo
that I am not on the fucking menu.

I guess no one bothered to tell you
that I am not an afternoon snack.

I guess no one explained to you
that women are not here for your convenience.

I burn rubber out of the lot,
your swagger an accusation in my rear-view mirror,
your departing whistle like the report of a rifle,

the taste of my food soured
by the pungency of your aggression,
my ten minutes of leisure destroyed
by the tastelessness of your rabid onslaught.

Putting Your Penis in a Box

Let's talk about the 'friend zone':
that's the box you put your penis into
when you're too chicken to speak out
because women are not fucking mind readers.

Let's talk about being 'cock blocked':
that's the wall that goes up for our defense
when you behave like a fucking prick
because women don't have to put up with your bullshit.

Let's talk about being 'pussy whipped':
that's the cage you put yourself into
when you let your cock make the decisions for you
because women can't magically take away your free will.

These constructs are the nightmares
of a patriarchal society, they force our minds
into patterns that damage our souls, like a woman who
feels the need to 'keep her man's balls in her purse',
can't resist trapping a boyfriend with a lie,
uses sex as a weapon to snare a 'sugar daddy',
toys with her tadpole just because a 'cougar' can do that.

Let's face it, after a lifetime of hearing men talk smack about
punting the cunt—
wetting their dick—
beating them guts—
doing a sloppy—
banging a side piece—
hitting a dime—
getting some skank—
tagging a whore—
how do you expect us to behave?

We have been battered so badly
that now all we know how to do is scheme.

We bear the brunt of our own pain
battling each other until walking into a room
of women is like walking into an arena of gladiators.

How dirty must the patriarchs of our society
have trained us to play if this is the level
of viciousness upon which we choose to stand?

So let's talk about lies where
women who 'give out' are 'sluts'
and those who don't are 'bitches'.

Let's talk about fairy-tales
where men are white knights
who are supposed to rescue women.

Let's talk about myths
where men are free to sew
as many wild oats as they'd like,
but women must be virgins on wedding nights
in pristine white dresses no one could ever keep spotless.

These constructs are the nightmares
of a patriarchal society that force our minds
into patterns damaging to our souls
when all we have to do is change the language,
and we will shatter the boxes,
break down the walls,
and unlock all the cages.

Goddess

It took me a long time to take this title. After all, I had never had a goddess image after which to mold myself.

I had tried being nice. I had tried playing with the boys. I had tried beating society at its own games. Nothing had worked.

So one day, I realized there was a way out: I could rise above it. I could recognize my own independence. I could tell the truth about my past. I could come out to the world as a flawed heterosexual and sexually active female who had been scarred and scared many times. I could have a heart and a relationship and still have my independence and my freedom.

Using the word 'goddess' does not mean I think women are deities and males are not, it simply means that I accept there are strong images of women who are much more than unrealistic, virginal versions of real women. It means that I reject all ideals of the patriarchy and I understand I do not have to fit into any generalized molds to exist. It means I understand that playing dirty by using my own physical and sexual attributes to 'get ahead' is not the way to empower my gender either.

Feminists come from all cultures and all walks of life. We all want different things, but what we have in common is that we want to choose those things and we want to live in a world without a patriarchy. Sure, some of us might toy with the idea of a matriarchy as a just dessert for society, but most of us know that equality (for men, women, and transgender) is the only right answer.

To me, to embrace the goddess is to reject concepts of a monotheistic, male-based society. It is to reject all stereotypical concepts of gender. I am not against using phrases like 'pussy power' or 'my uterus my right' because women, people born with female body parts, have been silenced for thousands of years. I believe we have a right to proudly say words associated with our bodies, but I also believe that we will only find equality if we work with all genders to break stereotypes directly associated with possessing either a vagina or a penis.

These poems are one way I try to give voice to the struggles and triumphs of real life women and all people who identify as women.

Magic Trick

You said, "I will love you forever,"
as if I had never heard that, your
head cocked to one side,
tawny eyes widening when

I couldn't believe in your magic.

I wanted to believe you—
I wanted, just that once,
to leap from your black hat
and find out if you could conjure me wings,

instead I reached out and slipped
a sable lock behind your ear.

Eventually, you bewitched me,
your voice a husky murmur,
hands a fine-spun spell latching
onto my hips so your tongue
could beguile my denial.

I had been hypnotized
by your body speaking in metaphors
and your mouth chanting hyperbole—

and now here we are, my U-Haul packed.

I am left like Pandora— bereft
after opening your box of secrets
to find your sorcery nothing but slight-of-hand

while you look down on me from your porch
as if my love has ruined your trick,
you alone in your spotlight, your charms exposed.

Maybe I didn't sprout wings,
but I won't need any voodoo
to put me back together again
or to know you did teach me the secret of flight—

just stand on my own two feet and leap.

I am witch.

The goddesses call me warrior,
their fierceness the serrated edges of my tongue;
Hecate claims me as sister,
her spells binding ink to my pages;
the Horned God bids me call him lover,
his recklessness coloring my mortality.

I am witch.

Seducing thunder with the sway of my hips,
sipping sunlight pooled between buildings,
supping on moonlight caught in rooftop eaves,
surfing summer squalls on my broomstick,
snickering as you paint eggs and trim trees.

I am witch.

Daydreams you never admit to having,
fantasies you hide behind religious facade—
the sunny liquid of my lips intoxicating you,
the moonlit morsels on my fingertips addicting you.

I am witch.

Know me as the goddess who birthed you, the woman
who would be called your equal, and the mother
who will raise daughters and sons in her image.

Black and Skulls

Today a coworker said,
"You have a lot of black clothes with skulls on them these days.
Is that some kind of a theme?"

I should have said that's right, it is:
I'm a single mother of twins
and their father turned out to be a deadbeat
so the black and skulls are kinda my thing right now.

I can find my own way in life,
but it's not easy to provide for kids
while the other parent gets away nearly scot-free
for a grand total of $168 a month
that the department of family services
may or may not be able to collect
in six to twelve months from,
whenever I call to ask them how my case is going.

That kinda makes my moods dark and my thoughts macabre
so, yeah, I wear a lot of black and skulls these days.

I should have said how
I'm not sure any amount of my love
will wash away the lies their father told,
I'm not sure any amount of my emotional support
will lessen the stress they see from single parenthood,
I'm not sure any amount of accolades at work
will ever add up to enough money for my children,
and I'm sure no amount of effort will make me enough
to make up for their father abandoning them.

So, yeah, black and skulls are kinda my thing these days.

I could have said how I'm addicted to the family dynamic on
NCIS, and how, when everything is finally done for the day,
I curl up with a daughter under each arm to watch it,
how the three of us form a heart-shaped cocoon of solidarity,

how I would give up my life if it would give them more,
how, despite everything, I still feel I am lucky,
how my daughters want to be scientists like their favorite NCIS
character,
how my clothes are Goth like that character, a symbol
for the strength I have gained and the pride I have found.

So, yeah, I kinda revel in wearing black and skulls.

But my coworker would judge me for not giving a pretty
answer, so I smile and say, "I'm fine, just expanding
Halloween,"
while I think how she doesn't deserve to understand
why I rock black and skulls most days this November.

Single Mother

The sounds of milk being guzzled and smacking lips
as one or the other of my twin girls snuggle closer,
warmth and softness seeping through the blanket into me.

I am lulled by the stillness that drapes the walls of my loft,
at two a.m. sounds drift only intermittently from the streets below
as downtown bars close and a deluge of party-goers
spill raucously onto sidewalks wrapped in bands of light and
shadow.

Chaotic hilarity echoes discordantly against concrete
followed by the sounds of street sweepers revving up
to clear out trash behind the dispersing crowds.

Those were the sounds that once claimed me,
the streets where I shut down night clubs with friends,
the breath of early mornings in which we celebrated our
freedom.

Now it only registers as a backdrop, an alien realm
when juxtaposed with the serenity of late night feedings
and a new world smelling of formula and diaper cream.

The Trappings of Clothing

My four year old daughters
run around naked for hours,
unashamed of their bodies,
creatures of nature
who are at ease in their skin
        because clothing traps them.

It is only us girls
and I cannot bring myself
to curb their natural inclinations,
because once they put on clothing
and don the expectations of society
        there will be no turning back.

My girls will never know again
what it is like to be shameless,
they will never know again
what it is like to walk without fear,
they will never feel again the air
        against their skin and smile.

I listen to their whimsical play
picturing their lithe bodies,
human beings who are works of art,
knowing I must shut down their innocence,
teaching them that society
        will view their skins as dangerous.

One day I must murder their self-confidence
by making them cower beneath strips of cloth,
then they will view the human form with trepidation,
see the prospect of nakedness with mortification,
look down at their magnificent bodies
        and instead of seeing artistry, see only flaws.

Merida

You tried to tame me like every other princess on the shelf.

You tried to fit me into societal standards
of what you think a girl should be.

You tried smoothing my unruly locks,
subduing my flaming hair,
sliming my obvious curves,
swabbing my face with makeup,
swathing me in frilly dresses,
suspending me like a puppet.

You tried to sell me to little girls
as a watered down version of what a real girl should be.

I like my hair curly and unkempt
because it plays with the wind as I run—

I like my face free of pastel paint
so my freckles will show, tokens
of sun kisses I earned through
my own sweat and tears—

I like my outfits flowing freely
because then I can draw enough breath
to sing loudly when the rain drenches my skin—

I won't sit properly like a dog trained to commands,
but rather I will lounge in whatever stance I prefer
like an equal with a will of my own.

I am a real woman
and I refuse to contort my soul into your square box
with cheap cellophane packaging

lining pink shelves in every toy store in America
demoted to stand with all the play kitchens
and doll babies and toy irons and vacuum cleaners.

I will never sell myself
to teach little girls that they
should be less than little boys.

I refuse to muzzle my mouth
and curb my wildness.

I will not march to the beat
of all the pliable dolls before me,
a sexist stereotype that breaks the backbones
of little girls before they can even stand.

I am not sugar and spice and everything nice.

I am fiery laughter and booming intellect and raging passion.

I am a real girl and I
am here to fucking stay.

My Mother's Voice

"That's not ladylike," my mother's voice.

She taught me to sit with legs primly crossed,
to speak softly with words that would not offend,
my spirited temperament an affront to her sensibilities.

"You'll never get a husband if you can't cook better."

She pushed upon me life as a wife and mother,
forcing me to leave home far too young,
tripping over myself to escape domestic drudgery.

"That doesn't accentuate your best features."

Through the years the chasm has widened,
a mother with no comprehension
of a daughter who fights for equality.

"That's not ladylike," my mother's voice,
the impetus for everything I have become.

Family Tree

My mother's brother always told the tale
Of how my grandfather was the trunk,
While his forefathers were the roots
And how men fed and watered the family organism.

The one son of my grandfather's loins
Deemed himself a hearty branch,
And when his only son was born
He christened him Leaf—
The parts that perpetuate a tree's existence.

But when I think of family,
I see my grandmother, Boudica-like,
Clothed in a short and spare frame,
I see my mother, dark and contentious
But never at a loss for words,
I hear the sound of lilting laughter,
The cadence of feminine voices raised to chivvy or defend.

In the homes of my family,
It is the silent resilience of my grandmother,
The fervor of perfumed hugs and handmade delicacies;
And the indomitable vigor of each of my aunts,
That nourished my family tree.

It has always been the women
Tilling the earth,
Forging the seeds,
Shaping the saplings,
And harvesting the fruit.

Good Day to Die

It was a good day to die— the day the blood came in rivers
That separated the children from the warriors.

It was a day fated no matter how we dragged our feet—
Our grandmother's enveloping us in their powdery scent
Exclaiming over how quickly we had sprung up,
Our mothers preening prettily amongst their friends,
Our rite of passage bestowing them with bragging rights.

While we saw only crimson— redness we could never forget
Because it would come back with every moon
Until we grew acclimated to the ribbons of red.

It was a good day to die— we had been unleashed into a
conflict That aging grandmother's and docile mothers
Have never been able to prepare daughters for.

As the flow of red rivers dictated our lives, we learned to exult in
it, Dividing ourselves between those who gave in
And supplicated themselves to the system
Versus those who would rather live as warriors
And shake the world with their fury—

We became berserkers crazed by the redness
Flowing from our bodies, while swearing our daughters
Would be freed by these rivers and not drown in them.

In the patriarchy, we are sacrificed for war at twelve years old
— Forty years later, we will be ripped from battle,
Finding us unrecognizable, even to ourselves.

Wasted

You waste your life with nights
too drunk to function. Passed
out, oblivion finds you, yet peace
eludes— a ghost touching
the edge of your mind.

There was the broken heart,
a childhood sweetheart,
shattering your ideal love.

There is the career,
not what it had promised.

There will be the future
stretching unyieldingly.

Time had already molded
your downfall, yet when I
first knew you, your soul
peeped out of a seam, fluttering
with a hint of radiance.

I saw promise spreading
before you, making me offer
myself to your lust, but now
your disillusions have twisted joy
into cruelty, your addictions
dimming your brightness.

What you have become is repulsive,
squandering yourself with drugs
and cheap lovers, till I cannot hold
onto the image of your beauty—
your dark hole too much for me.

I tell you I can no longer offer
what you seek. You call me bitch
and whore and traitor
because I will not sacrifice
myself to feed the creature
you have become,
because I will not suicide
my integrity to crawl
inside your singularity.

Nothing

I figured it out—
what makes me
avoid your calls,
lose your texts,
delete your emails,
      self-pleasure without you.

The thing is,
you throw yourself
down for me,
you besiege me,
draping your nakedness
      on every piece of my furniture—

or you are
manhandling me
while I clean house,
slapping my ass
while I wash dishes,
as if you think
      I am yours to accost—

or you are
sexting me
when I am in the middle
of a stressful workday,
shoving your desires
upon me by randomly
      sending shots of your penis—

you offer me
no challenge,
no mystery,

no depth,
no esteem,
no intellectual stimulation,
      NO sense of timing—

what I wanted was
a sliver of your heart,
the measure of your soul,
a symbiosis with your thoughts,
some acknowledgement of my worth
      because your dick signifies nothing.

While He Sleeps

He sleeps— sated and soft
his member spent
as his empires languish.

He had been dominant,
on top and in control
for thousands of years
while she lay awake,
plotting how best to gain
her power in his weakness.

She watched him,
and though she loved him,
she remained wedded to her plots.

He had refused to give
a voice to her. Once
or twice she had forged
weapons to rise against him,
yet he had defamed her,
stamping her marks
from the pages of history.

But time and lust
had delivered him again
and this time, while he slept
naively secure in his prowess,
she would change the tide
and make her victory stick.

Clubbing

You look at me like I am an object—
your hungry eyes rake my body from head to toe
simply because I am dressed
in red stilettos and a black mini skirt,
makeup immaculate,
hair twirled into a loose up-do,
a drink in my hand.

To you this means I am ripe for the taking
simply a passive female you hunger to sully —
so you may come onto me proffering a drink,
or sidle up behind me as I stand with friends,
or press your hardened dick against my ass as I dance.

You think your needs more important than mine—
that you have the right to ravage me
with your mind and your eyes and your hands and your penis,
smudging my independence with your forceful inclinations.

I am bragging rights...a conquest...a slut...a whore...
a being worth less than you are in your mind.

The hip hop club mix slams through the throbbing space
and quotes things that a man and a woman can do together,
lust vibrates through my veins with a sweet liquor buzz.

Just because the swing of my hips echoes the beat
does not imply it's okay for strange men to manhandle me—
just because I dress to accentuate my figure
does not imply I am unintelligent—
just because I am a sexual being
does not mean I am yours for the taking.

I will back away from you,
forced to seek cover from your invasion
across the dance floor with friends or near a bouncer.

Maybe I will go home with a respectful admirer
or maybe I will go home alone,
but I will be the one to make the choice
with my human rights, just the same as you.

Wanted

Ink slipping
across paper,

the scritch
of ball point
on vellum,

the slur
of moist cursive
against a slick page,

breathy exhalations
in pointed imagery,

scintillating gyrations
in curvy syntax,

lusty sighs
in figurative language,

poignant aches crouched
in every punctuation mark,

my need,
an empty page
yearning for one
skillful coauthor.

Stable

I will never curb my wildness again—
at least that is what I always swear, right before I
fall head over heels with someone new,
start craving his presence when I am sleepless,
think about what he would say to the silly things I do,
start sending a crazy mix of dirty love texts.

And then I let him tame me, let him
slide into the middle of my life,
mingle his dirty laundry with all of mine,
leave his toiletries all over the vanity and tub,
arrange kitchen cabinets and rearrange the fridge,
steer our steamy sex into sweet intimacy.

I swear I will never wear a halter again, then I
play jump rope with my heartstrings,
finger-paint with love while hope doodles outside the lines,
drop my loneliness off at the curb and wave it goodbye,
grab my luggage off the conveyor belt and start to unpack,
slip his love over my head like a silky chemise.

I swore I would never do this again, never
let love out of her stall and off of her rope,
make my heart stand still for a bridle and saddle,
allow emotion to take hold of the reins.
This time I was positive I would never take the bit again,
yet I have made myself into a liar
every morning we say we will be on time
but make love in the soft glow of dawn;
those evenings we are exhausted,
but stay awake lost in the lilt of our voices;
each time I share more of my savage pieces
and willingly enter the stable
our arms build around each other.

Run

The air, a lover, sliding his fingers
across my neck and bare midriff
as I press my feet to the concrete,
bringing into bear my focus.

Resolve propels me along the busy sidewalk
as dusk drapes herself across my shoulders
and the ideas that chase me fall in pitch to a low hum,
stress sliding away in a shimmer of sweet sweat.

Soon it is only me and the fallen night,
I become ephemeral, outpacing reality,
until I turn a corner between buildings
and the air becomes an aggressor,
pressing himself against my momentum.

With every block my will strengthens,
I now must become a warrior,
pushing forward as street lamps pop on,
turning the final corner at a stop light,
and sprinting the last block home.

colophon

Brought to you by Wider Perspectives Publishing, care of Tanya
Cunningham-Jones and James Wilson with the mission of advancing
the poetry and creative community of Hampton Roads, Virginia.

See our production of the works of
 Tanya Cunningham (Scientific Eve)
 Ray Simmons
 Taz Waysweete'
 Bobby K. (The Poor Man's Poet)
 J. Scott Wilson (TEECH!)
 Jorge Mendez & JT Williams
 Terra Leigh
 S.A. Borders-Shoemaker
 Kenneth Sutton (the Bard of Machipongo)
 Edith Blake
THE Hampton Roads Artistic Collective
and others to come soon.

We promote and support the artists of the 757
from the seats, from the stands,
from the snapping fingers and clapping hands
from the pages, and the stages
and now we pass them forth to the ages

Stop it James, just stop it!

Check for the above artists on FaceBook, the Virginia Poetry
Online channel on YouTube, and the Hampton Roads Artistic
Collective webpage.
Hampton Roads Artistic Collective is the non-profit extension
of WPP and strives to simultaneously support worthy causes in
Hampton Roads and the creative artists.

www.ingramcontent.com/pod-product-compliance
Lightning Source LLC
Chambersburg PA
CBHW060514280326
41933CB00014B/2963